MAY 2017

Moe's Toes Froze

Kelly Doudna

Consulting Editor, Diane Craig, M.A./Reading Specialist

ABDO
Publishing Company

Published by ABDO Publishing Company, 4940 Viking Drive, Edina, Minnesota 55435.

Printed in the United States.

Credits
Edited by: Pam Price
Curriculum Coordinator: Nancy Tuminelly
Cover and Interior Design and Production: Mighty Media
Photo Credits: BananaStock Ltd., Brand X Pictures, Comstock, Eyewire Images, Hemera, Image 100, Image Source, PhotoDisc, Rubberball Productions

Library of Congress Cataloging-in-Publication Data

Doudna, Kelly, 1963-
    Moe's toes froze / Kelly Doudna.
        p. cm. -- (Rhyme time)
    Includes index.
    ISBN 1-59197-805-X (hardcover)
    ISBN 1-59197-911-0 (paperback)
    1. English language--Rhyme--Juvenile literature. I. Title. II. Rhyme time (ABDO Publishing Company)

PE1517.D687 2004
428.1'3--dc22

                                                                        2004047360

SandCastle™ books are created by a professional team of educators, reading specialists, and content developers around five essential components that include phonemic awareness, phonics, vocabulary, text comprehension, and fluency. All books are written, reviewed, and leveled for guided reading, early intervention reading, and Accelerated Reader® programs and designed for use in shared, guided, and independent reading and writing activities to support a balanced approach to literacy instruction.

Let Us Know

After reading the book, SandCastle would like you to tell us your stories about reading. What is your favorite page? Was there something hard that you needed help with? Share the ups and downs of learning to read. We want to hear from you! To get posted on the ABDO Publishing Company Web site, send us e-mail at:

sandcastle@abdopub.com

SandCastle Level: Fluent

Words that rhyme do not have to be spelled the same. These words rhyme with each other:

chose

hose

doze

nose

elbows

pose

froze

rose

goes

toes

Marcus likes to lie in the grass and **doze**.

Becky **chose** a french fry to eat.

Hannah and her family played in the snow so long they almost froze.

Jake sprays his friends with
the hose.

Nora raises her arms so her face is between her **elbows**.

Joanie smiles at her dad when
he rubs her **nose**.

Josh often goes fishing with his grandpa.

Wes and his parents pose for a family picture.

Nadia and Donna sit in the sun and wiggle their bare **toes**.

It is Tim's mom's birthday.

He is going to give her a
red rose.

Moe's Toes Froze

Moe went outside
and struck a pose.

He knew that he
should have worn
warm clothes.

He stood still so long
that he began to doze.

This was just
the start of Moe's
winter woes.

Along came Rose
with Joe's
garden hose.

ROSE
MOE'S PAL
WITH JOE'S
HOSE

It was December,
so the water
soon froze.

16

At first it froze
on Moe's
poor toes.

The next things that froze
were Moe's elbows.

Moe's nose was the last thing that froze.

When Moe woke up,
he went inside
for some warm,
comfy clothes.

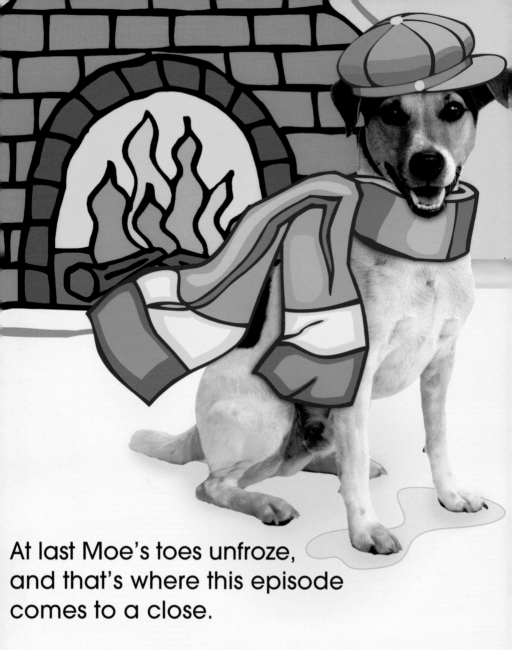

At last Moe's toes unfroze,
and that's where this episode
comes to a close.

Rhyming Riddle

What do you call a sleeping position?

Doze pose

Glossary

doze. to sleep lightly

episode. one in a series of loosely connected stories or events

freeze. to became chilled with cold; to become solid ice from being in the cold

pose. to hold a position while a picture is taken; a position or attitude taken for artistic reasons or to impress others

woe. a huge trouble or problem

About SandCastle™

A professional team of educators, reading specialists, and content developers created the SandCastle™ series to support young readers as they develop reading skills and strategies and increase their general knowledge. The SandCastle™ series has four levels that correspond to early literacy development in young children. The levels are provided to help teachers and parents select the appropriate books for young readers.

Emerging Readers
(no flags)

Beginning Readers
(1 flag)

Transitional Readers
(2 flags)

Fluent Readers
(3 flags)

These levels are meant only as a guide. All levels are subject to change.

To see a complete list of SandCastle™ books and other nonfiction titles from ABDO Publishing Company, visit www.abdopub.com or contact us at:
4940 Viking Drive, Edina, Minnesota 55435 • 1-800-800-1312 • fax: 1-952-831-1632